# IF YOU WERE A
# DOG

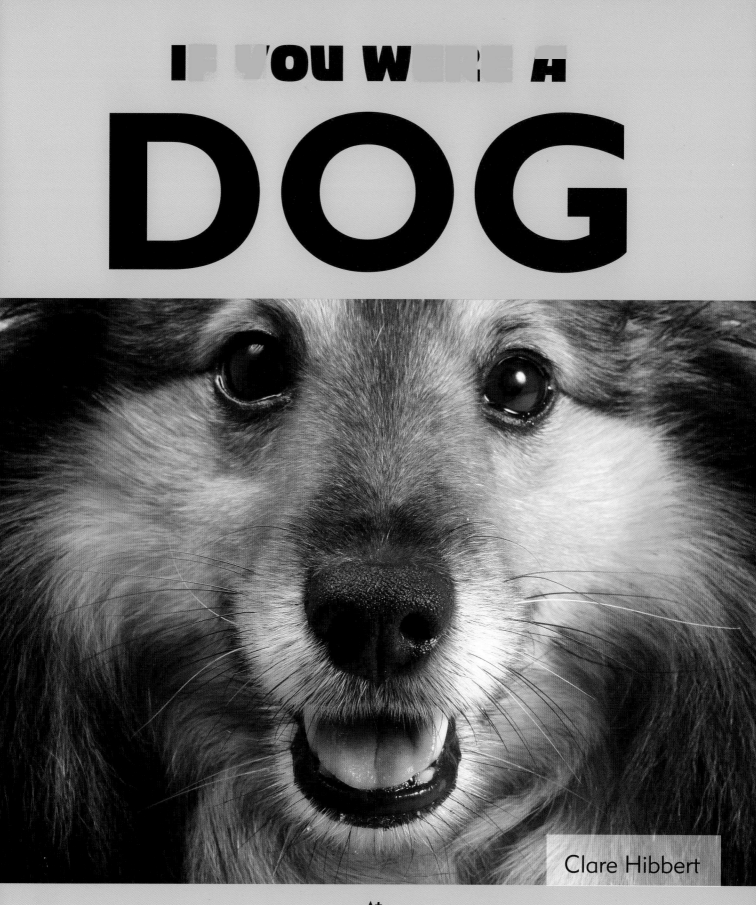

Clare Hibbert

Smart Apple Media

Published in the United States by Smart Apple Media
PO Box 3263, Mankato, Minnesota 56002

Copyright © Arcturus Holdings Limited

The right of Clare Hibbert to be identified as the author of this work has been asserted by her in
accordance with the Copyright, Designs and Patents Act 1988.

Editor: Joe Harris
Picture researcher: Clare Hibbert
Designer: Emma Randall

Picture credits:
All images Shutterstock except 5 (main) Ramona Richter/Tierfotoagentur/FLPA.

Library of Congress Cataloging-in-Publication Data

Hibbert, Clare, 1970-
 If you were a dog / Clare Hibbert.
    p. cm. --  (If you were a--)
 Audience: Grade 4 to 6.
 Summary: "Describes the features, life, and habits of dogs in contrast to human life"-- Provided by
publisher.
 Includes bibliographical references and index.
 ISBN 978-1-59920-960-9 (library binding)
 1.  Dogs--Juvenile literature. 2.  Dogs--Behavior--Juvenile literature.  I. Title. II. Title: Dog.
 SF426.5.H529 2014
 636.7--dc23
                          2013002950

Printed in the United States

Supplier 02, Date 0814, Print Run 3766
SL002675US

98765432

# Contents

# Sight, Sound, and Touch

If you were a dog, you'd see and hear the world differently from humans. You would be better at finding your way around at dawn and dusk, when there is only faint light. You would also be able to pick up sounds that are outside the range of human hearing.

## How Dogs See

Cones are the parts of the eye's retina that sense color and detail. Dogs have ten times fewer cones than us, and they see the world in only blues and yellows. However, their retinas have more rods than ours. Rods are the parts of the retina that see the best in dim light.

## Range of Vision

Different breeds have different ranges of vision, depending on where the dog's eyes are on the head. A typical dog can see 250 degrees around its head, compared to a human's range of about 180 degrees.

## Dog Questions

**Q: Do dog whistles really work?**
A: Dog whistles produce a sound that dogs can hear but humans can't. Dogs can hear twice the range of frequencies that humans can. They are better at hearing over distances, too—four times better than us!

## Feelers

Dogs have whiskers around their muzzle and above their jaw. These feelers help dogs with their sense of touch and their "spatial awareness"—for instance, being able to tell if they can fit through a narrow gap in a fence.

# A World of Smell

If you were a dog, you'd have a keen sense of smell. Your wild cousins, wolves, use smell for hunting, but you don't need to track down your food. You would use smell to check out your surroundings, to communicate with other dogs, and even to sense people's emotions.

## Super Sniffers
A dog's sense of smell is far more impressive than a human's. A bloodhound's nose has around 230 million scent cells, and a German shepherd's nose has 220 million. A person's nose has just five million scent cells.

## Smelly Messages
Dogs learn a lot about their surroundings through their noses. Out on a walk, they are always pausing to sniff and find out which other dogs have been there and whose territory they are in. Dogs mark their territory with strong-smelling urine and feces.

## Dog Detectives

Dogs are great at tracking, so we use them to find missing people. They can pick up the "trail" scent of someone lost or a criminal on the run, even when it is days old. Dogs also help to find survivors after disasters.

## Dog Questions

Q: Can dogs smell emotions?
A: Dogs can smell certain chemicals that people give off. For example, people (and dogs) secrete a hormone called cortisol when they are afraid.

# Chasing and Herding

If you were a dog, you'd be a bundle of energy—eager to chase and track, and equipped with excellent senses to help you do just that. Your wild ancestors, wolves, herded animals when hunting as a pack, and you would have that instinct, too.

## Champion Speedsters

The fastest dogs—greyhounds and Salukis—were bred to catch rabbits and hares. If they spot one, they cannot resist chasing it! They can race along at 40 mph (60 kph). Most dogs, though, are built for staying power, not speed.

## Helpful Herders

Some dogs have been bred to help farmers look after their livestock. Collies, sheepdogs, cattle dogs, and mountain dogs all have a keen herding instinct and are intelligent, too. They can control sheep, goats, or even cattle.

## Sheepdog Skills

At sheepdog trials, herding dogs can show off their skills. The exact challenges vary, but usually the dogs must drive the sheep around an obstacle course and into a pen, and also separate one or more animals from the rest.

## Dog Questions

**Q: Why do some dogs chase cats?**
A: Most dogs will run after anything that moves—balls, cars, people, rabbits, squirrels, and of course, cats. Experts call dogs' thrill of the chase the "prey drive"—it is their natural urge to chase after, or hunt, prey.

# Walks!

If you were a dog, going for a walk would be the highlight of your day. You would look forward to investigating interesting smells, finding fun things to chase, and meeting other dogs. But best of all, you would be spending time with your favorite companion— your owner!

## Why Walk?

Dogs need their daily exercise—and they love it, too. Many become terrifically excited when they hear the word "walk"! Some dogs even drop not-so-subtle hints, such as bringing their leash to their owner or standing by the door.

## Meeting Friends

Walks are social occasions. Along the route, dogs meet other dogs and greet them by sniffing their faces and bottoms. Dogs remember other individual dogs by their unique smell, not their appearance.

## Dog Questions

Q: Why does my dog paw the path after he pees?
A: Dogs mark their territory with urine or feces (see page 6). Sometimes they scrape at the ground near the scent message. The claw marks help to draw the attention of other dogs to the smelly marker.

## Running Free

All dogs need to learn to walk calmly on a leash, but their favorite part of a "walk" is when they can run free. Dogs' bodies are designed for long-distance running. When they're off the leash, they get the chance to stretch their legs.

11

# Pack Animal

If you were a dog, you would have descended from wolves. You would still share many characteristics with your wild cousins. You would be very sociable, and when you were running or playing with other dogs, you would behave as if you were part of a pack.

## Knowing Their Place

For many years, experts believed that dog owners should be like the "top dog" of a wolf pack. Owners, they argued, should scold and punish their dogs to help them understand their pack "position" and be better behaved.

## Training Ideas

More recently, many experts have argued that relationships between pet dogs and people are different to those between wolves. Owners do not need to punish their pets into behaving well. Dogs respond better to rewards, praise, and affection.

## Pets Away!

The close relationship between pet dogs and their owners means that dogs, unlike pet cats, can feel "at home" anywhere. Going on vacation is an adventure for them, so long as their human family comes, too.

### Dog Questions

Q: What if a new dog joins the family?
A: Dog–dog relationships are different to dog–human ones and closer to how wolves interact. When a new dog or puppy arrives, the animals must figure out who is the "top dog".

# Dog "Talk"

If you were a dog, you'd be able to bark and make other noises. You would use these sounds to communicate. Your voice would allow you to demand things you needed or wanted, as well as to warn of danger or help those around you in other ways.

## Barking

Dogs bark to sound an alarm. Pet dogs bark when they sense an intruder. In the wild, dogs do it to let other dogs know about approaching danger. Dogs also bark to challenge other dogs—or simply when they are overexcited.

### Dog Questions

Q: Why does my dog growl when I give it a bone?
A: Dogs growl if they have something that they don't want to share. The sound sends a clear message: "Back off, and don't you dare think of trying to steal this treat from me!"

### Howling

Wolves howl to communicate with each other over long distances. The pack can keep track of each other, and it can also communicate with other packs. Pet dogs howl to express worry or anxiety, for instance, if their owners are away.

### Whimpering

Puppies whimper as a sign of friendliness. Grown dogs will whimper for attention or to comfort themselves when they are lonely or in pain. The whining sound dogs make when begging is different from whimpering.

# Body Language

If you were a dog, your body language would be just as important for communicating as the noises you made. Your head, body, and tail would all speak volumes—not only to other dogs but also to the people around you. Body language would reveal your state of mind.

## Tail Lalk

Dogs' tails are very expressive. Dogs wag them enthusiastically when they are feeling friendly and contented. Dogs that are doing things they enjoy, such as running or playing games, usually hold their tails upright.

### Dog Questions

Q: Why does my dog lick my face?
A: Pups lick their mothers' faces to prompt them to regurgitate food, which the pups can eat. Dogs do the same to their owners, who are a little like parents to them. They know their owners won't regurgitate food, though!

## Threat Display

Dogs can be very aggressive sometimes. When they want to frighten off a rival, they bare their teeth and stare their opponent in the eye. At the same time, their hackles (neck hairs) rise.

## The Meek Dog

Most dogs try to avoid getting into fights with bigger, more powerful dogs. The best way is to adopt a submissive pose. The signs of submission include ears moving back, eyes looking away, and body and tail held low.

# Dog Feelings

If you were a dog, you wouldn't feel the same all the time. You would react to events and to the emotions of those around you. Sometimes you'd feel grumpy, sometimes you might feel frightened, and other times you would feel joyful and excited.

## Feeling "Love"

Dogs long for human company and approval—but can this come from just anyone? It seems not. Pets pine for owners who die or go away, so doggy affection clearly amounts to more than just "puppy love".

## Scary Stuff

Most dogs are frightened of thunderstorms and fireworks— they dislike the loud bangs and flashes of light. Dogs who are frightened flatten their ears, lower their tails, and slink low to the ground.

## Dog Questions

Q: Can dogs feel guilt?
A: Seventy-four percent of dog owners think their dogs can feel guilt, but experts are not so sure. A "guilty" dog avoids eye contact—behavior that is more likely to be the dog trying to keep a low profile in response to the owner's mood.

18

### Conquering Fears

Sometimes dogs, especially shelter dogs, are fearful because they were mistreated in the past. With time and patience, their fears can usually be overcome, but some dogs may never feel secure in certain situations.

# Training

If you were a dog, you'd be eager to learn and fit in. You would understand a range of basic commands. You would know what to do partly by recognizing the words themselves, but also by "reading" your owner's tone of voice and body language.

## Voice Commands

The five basic commands for dogs are "Sit," "Stay," "Come," "Down," and "Heel." However, many dogs learn to recognize more instructions than these. The trick for the owner is to make each command sound as different as possible.

## Rewards for Obedience

Owners need to say their commands clearly so that their animals have a chance of understanding them. They should also reward good behavior, either with a treat or by praising and petting.

## Bad Behavior

Dogs are most likely to do things their owners don't want them to when they are bored. Smart owners avoid giving them the opportunity to misbehave. They make sure that a space is "dog-proof" before leaving their pet there unsupervised.

## Dog Questions

**Q: Why does my dog chew?**
A: Puppies chew to explore the world and soothe their itchy gums when they're teething. Adult dogs chew because they like it! Giving pets toys made of hard rubber or rawhide will stop them from chewing favorite belongings.

# Mealtimes

If you were a dog, you'd probably eat two meals a day. You'd prefer eating at the same times each day, so you knew when to expect your food. You'd also need fresh drinking water—about two-and-a-half times as much water, by volume, as food.

## Doggy Diet

Dogs are carnivores, or meat-eaters. They like nothing better than gnawing meat off a bone. Pet dogs get most of their meat from canned food, which also contains cereals. Crunchy biscuits keep their teeth and gums healthy.

### Dog Questions

Q: Is it OK to feed my dog between meals?
A: Obesity is a common problem for dogs—more than two-fifths of dogs in the United States are obese. Limiting food to mealtimes makes it easier to stop from dogs overeating.

## Teeth for the Job

The four sharp teeth that wild dogs use to kill prey are called canines. (The word *canine* also means a member of the dog family.) At the back of the mouth, dogs have larger, flatter teeth that are good at tearing up flesh.

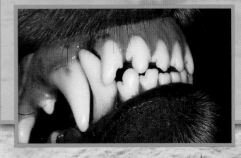

## Taste

Dogs have only 1,700 taste buds, compared to a human's 9,000. Most are at the tip of the tongue. Dogs distinguish between bitter, sweet, salty, and sour flavors—and like us, some dogs have a very sweet tooth!

# Care for Fur

If you were a dog, you'd have a fur coat to keep you warm. You'd groom yourself by licking—and would have some help from your owner, too. You wouldn't be able to sweat, so if your cozy coat made you too hot, you'd pant to let heat escape and cool yourself down.

## Hairstyles

There are around 200 different breeds of dog and many different hairstyles. Dogs can have short, long, straight, or curly fur. Fancy coats that are especially long or curly need lots of brushing and looking after.

## Clean Coats

Although dogs groom themselves, they also need help from their owners. Regular brushing helps to keep coats sleek and strengthens the bond between owner and dog. Sometimes dogs will need bathing, too.

## Dog Questions

Q: Why does my dog roll in smelly things?
A: Many dogs roll in fox feces, rotting matter, or other stinky stuff. They might do it to disguise their own scent from prey— or just because it's fun and they love strong smells!

## Itching and Scratching

A dog that is always scratching may have fleas. A vet can advise on the best way to stop fleas. Other parasites that can affect dogs include ticks (picked up on country walks) and worms.

# Puppy Development

If you were a dog, you'd have started life as a puppy. You would have spent your first two or three months with your mother, who would have fed you milk and kept you warm and clean. While you were a puppy, you'd have slept and played and learned the skills you'd need as a grown-up dog.

## Newborns

At first, puppies just sleep and feed. They whimper and jostle for position. Their eyes and ears stay closed for the first couple of weeks. The only sense the pups need is smell—so they can sniff out their mother's milk.

## Dog Questions

Q: Why does my puppy chase its tail?
A: Puppies love chasing games—they are good practice for hunting prey. If there are no brothers or sisters around to play chase with, a puppy will happily chase its own tail instead.

## Litter Mates

Small dogs may only have one or two puppies, but larger breeds may give birth to 20 or more. Playing with brothers and sisters is fun—and it teaches important life lessons, too, such as how to get along with others.

## Feeding Puppies

For the first three or four weeks, puppies only need milk. Then they can start to try solid food, such as biscuits. They continue drinking their mother's milk, though, until they are weaned at six to eight weeks old.

# Humans and Dogs

If you were a dog, you'd be used to getting along with humans—dogs have been doing so since they were first domesticated thousands of years ago. You'd be loyal to your owner, and you might even work as a companion for a living!

## Workers and Companions

Early humans found dogs useful because they helped them to hunt. People still use dogs as guard dogs or hunting dogs. Although they take on responsible jobs, dogs can be playful, too. Even an adult dog will adopt a puppyish pose when it wants to play.

## Dog Questions

Q: How should I approach a strange dog?
A: Dogs are usually friendly, but it's not a good idea to approach a dog you don't know. Ask its owner first. If they say it's OK, then you can crouch low and offer your hand for the dog to sniff.

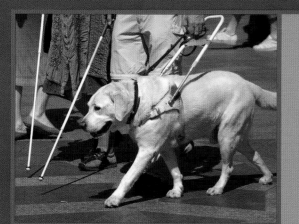

## Service Dogs

Dogs make great helpers. Some are trained to assist people who are blind, deaf, or in a wheelchair. Their amazing ability to smell chemical changes means dogs can even forewarn owners with epilepsy when they are about to have a seizure.

## Responsibilities

Dogs are part of the family. They live for 15 years or more, and owners have to care for them all that time—feeding them, walking them, and taking them to the vet. To prevent unwanted puppies, owners should also have their dogs neutered.

# Glossary

**ancestor** A member of the family that lived long ago.

**anxiety** Worry. Some dogs suffer from "separation anxiety"—stress when they are separated from their owners, for example, when they are out at school.

**breed** A class of dogs that look similar and have related ancestry, for example, golden retriever.

**carnivore** An animal whose diet is mostly meat. Most carnivorous mammals have four long, sharp teeth near the front of the mouth (canines) that are designed for tearing through flesh.

**domesticated** Describes an animal that is used to living alongside people, rather than in the wild.

**epilepsy** A condition that means sufferers sometimes lose consciousness or have convulsions (a seizure).

**hackles** Hairs on the back of a dog's neck that stand up when the animal is angry or alarmed.

**hormone** A substance released into the blood by a gland that changes how certain body cells behave. Cortisol is a hormone released by people and dogs when they are afraid.

**livestock** Animals kept by farmers, such as cattle, sheep, and pigs.

**muzzle** The protruding part of an animal's face that includes the nose and mouth.

**neutered** Describes an animal that has had an operation to remove its reproductive organs so that it cannot have young.

**obese** Extremely overweight—in dogs, obesity means being about 15 percent heavier than their ideal body weight.

**parasite** An animal that lives on another animal and relies on it for food.

**pine for** To miss and long for.

**prey** An animal that is hunted by other animals for food. Rabbits are typical prey for wild dogs.

**"puppy love"** Affection that is intense but relatively shallow.

**regurgitate** Spit up partly-chewed food. Mother dogs regurgitate meat for their puppies.

**responsibility** A task that someone has to perform as part of their job or because of their relationship to someone else.

**retina** The light-sensitive lining at the back of the eye that allows an animal to see.

**scent cells** Receptors in the nose that send signals to the brain, which then makes sense of that information allowing an animal to smell.

**spatial awareness** The ability to sense what is in the surrounding space.

**submissive** Meek.

**taste buds** Receptors in the mouth that send signals to the brain, which then makes sense of that information, allowing an animal to taste.

**territory** The area of land where an animal lives. Dogs mark their territory with urine or feces.

**weaned** Taken off mother's milk and put exclusively on solid foods.

## Further Reading

*Dogs and Puppies (100 Facts)* by Camilla de la Bedoyere (Miles Kelly Publishing, 2010)

*How to Speak Dog!* by Sarah Whitehead (Scholastic Reference, 2008)

*National Geographic Kids Everything Dogs: All the Canine Facts, Photos, and Fun You Can Get Your Paws On!* by Rebecca Baines (National Geographic Children's Books, 2012)

*Understanding Your Dog: The First Guide for Humans Written by a Dog* by Sue Day and Rocky (CreateSpace Independent Publishing Platform, 2011)

## Web Sites

http://animal.discovery.com/guides/dogs/dogs.html
A guide to dog care from the Animal Planet web site, with information on choosing a dog, dog life stages, dog health, and dog-proofing your home.

http://www.loveyourdog.com
A kids' guide to dog care, including tips on training.

http://www.aspca.org/Pet-care/dog-care
Learn about looking after your dog from the animal welfare charity, the ASPCA.

http://www.dogchannel.com/dog-breeds/
An A-to-Z guide to dog breeds from the Dog Channel.

http://www.akc.org
The official web site for the American Kennel Club, an organization that gives information and advice about dogs.

# Index